Crow Gulch

Crow Gulch

Douglas Walbourne-Gough

icehouse poetry
an imprint of Goose Lane Editions

Edited by Robin Richardson.
Cover and page design by Julie Scriver.
Interior cover image courtesy of Corner Brook Museum and Archives
Printed in Canada by Coach House.
10 9 8 7 6 5 4 3

Library and Archives Canada Cataloguing in Publication

Title: Crow Gulch / Douglas Walbourne-Gough.
Names: Walbourne-Gough, Douglas, 1982- author.
Description: Poems.
Identifiers: Canadiana 20190090715 | ISBN 9781773101019 (softcover)
Classification: LCC PS8645.A4555 C76 2019 | DDC C811/.6—dc23

Goose Lane Editions acknowledges the generous support of the Government of Canada, the Canada Council for the Arts, and the Government of New Brunswick.

Goose Lane Editions
500 Beaverbrook Court, Suite 330
Fredericton, New Brunswick
CANADA E3B 5X4
gooselane.com

A way to corner myself is what I want. Some blunt
  place I can't go
beyond. Where excuses stop.

— John Steffler

For my grandparents,
Ella Josephine Campbell and Rudolph Gough Sr.

Contents

Introduction

There was also Shacktown, a section of the west side where the very poor lived, and beyond that Crow Gulch which was the dumping ground for bums, bootleggers, and other less-mentionable outcasts.

— Percy Janes

During the construction of Corner Brook's pulp-and-paper mill, migrant workers came from all over Western Newfoundland in search of work. There were a few temporary encampments, dismantled and abandoned after the mill was complete. One, however, remained — Crow Gulch, a community that sat on the shore of the Bay of Islands, less than two kilometers west from downtown Corner Brook.

The Gulch was the site of an old slate quarry, less than hospitable. The gradient of the hill was severe, and there were large boulders throughout the site that outsized the homes. An operational CN railway line ran through the middle, and the community lacked such amenities as running water. In later years, some residents received electricity and telephone access, but only if they lived on the upper side of the tracks.

Social divisions, particularly those of class and race, arose between the people of Corner Brook and the surrounding communities. It seemed everyone wore stigma in some form or another, and Crow Gulch was no exception.

Many of the families who settled here were of Indigenous ancestry, and the common derogatory epithet for Indigenous people of mixed French and Mi'kmaq descent in southwestern Newfoundland was "jackatar."

Eventually, when the people of Crow Gulch were legally ushered from their homes, the majority moved into Corner Brook's first large-scale social-housing project, Dunfield Park. The last people to leave clung on until the late 1970s. Some say Crow Gulch persisted longer.

Crow Gulch sub-area is bounded on the north by the Humber Arm, on the west by a steep shoulder of Crow Hill which cuts the area off from any development towards Curling, on the South by Curling Highway and on the east by an undeveloped gap of some 350 feet which separates the area from the buildings on Pier Road. The area is characterized by small, inaccessible houses in very bad condition on a bare, precipitous hillside varying from 29% to 50% in gradient. Total clearance and abandonment as a residential area has been the consistent recommendation of all studies of Crow Gulch since 1955. It is the action proposed in this scheme.

Fraught

Folded, slick. Its weight a comfort
against Wi-Fi, modern uselessness.
A good knife laughs off plastic
cutlery from office-soft retirement
parties. Recalls cleaning fish, skinning
moose. Quietly proving itself.

Unfold the blade. Relish its click,
slight recoil. Click. Repeat until
the motion is familiar as a kiss.

Its steel is stainless, nondescript
but for one long, wise eye, thinnest
of thin-lipped grins. Tongue so sharp
it screamed heads clean off in France,
split March in half through Caesar's ribs.

Burnished handle offers warmth,
trust. Lulled by the intimacy of wood,
I almost forget — a knife is fraught
with urge, at odds with its edge.

Breaking Ground

What if the land you want to break is bedrock?
Bald fields of stone flowered with boulders, kissed
by bog and moss less than knee-deep? What if
this land is so stubborn, so resistant to charms
that spruce grow sideways, grow themselves
into knots for spite? What, then, is your next
move? How do you woo a stony place whose blood's
gone salt and spends half its year in snow?

A land so unfriendly that its dark and angry ocean
borders hold far more life at twice the risk of death
yet you set sail between continents to get there,
just to dock and take breaks between boatloads
of some other country's fish? Well, you buck up.
You defy law and logic, squat in tickles and coves,
learn their rhythms, make do along the edges. You learn
to take salt-blood as lover, as old god of giveth-and-
taketh-away. Bend like tuckamore, lean against
the wind, love it like a mother, let it shape you.

You keep going because refusing to accept it
means accepting death. Life here was that simple.
Over generations you grow a bit lower, closer
to Earth like cloudberries, like Labrador tea,
like crowberries and lichen. Become stocky
like black bears, cling to this rock as stubbornly
as it tries starving you out, tries drowning
your loved ones, tries blowing you off a cliff,
back across the Atlantic like a skipped stone.

Oral History: Q and A (I)

Q: Hmm, how about the origins
   of Crow Gulch, do you know where —

A: I have no idea. Like, I know what a gulch is.
   A gulch is, you know, I guess this unsavoury,
   unattractive hole in the Earth.

Q: Mhmmmm.

A: You know, it conjures images of flocks
   of crows hanging around a garbage dump...

Q: It's fairly ominous, yeah.

A: Yeah, I wouldn't want to go there.

Imposter

In airports, MacBooking in designer shoes, unnecessary scarf.
Looking good. Asked by fellow travellers if the Wi-Fi's working.
Some new, fleeting camaraderie. Feels odd but oddly good. Flash
my iPhone boarding pass with panache, feeling foreign about
being capable of this. Already learning the drill of security, un-
lacing boots and removing my belt before my turn. Laptop in its
own bin.

Jetting to Calgary, staying in Kitsilano on someone else's dime.
Pint of IPA with breakfast in Kelowna, sushi served from a model
train in Banff. Gondola rides and hot springs. Feeling European,
then realizing how fucked up that is. Banff Centre invader, em-
barrassed by my meal card. Spend most days hiding. Strange
dreams, major shakes in confidence.

Those mountains, though.

September 14, 1966

They spoke in low voices,
obvious they had been to train
derailments before, yet
there was a stoop to their shoulders
and their heads bowed.

The pitch-black night
added little consolation
to anyone. There were few
sounds. Someone tapped
the wheel of an overturned
flatcar. CNR

officials huddled together
near the remains, one
of the dead men entangled
in the torn and twisted steel.
Stretcher bearers carried
the bodies and the injured
along the track toward Pier Rd.

Thomas Fitzpatrick, 37, Michael
Murphy, 55, and Duncan Henderson,
32, all of Corner Brook, killed when
an empty boxcar immediately behind
the engine slammed into the locomotive
and sheared off the cab.

7:10 p.m., all three men in the diesel
engine of a fourteen-car switcher
on a run from Curling, it collided

with No. 203, a westbound mixed
mail-express train that left the station
for Port aux Basques only 10 minutes

before those few split seconds
of the inanimate gone wild.

Definition

jackatar, n also jackie tar,
jackitar, jack-o-tar, jackotaw, jacky tar.

– Appellation for common sailor.

– A Newfoundlander of mixed French and Micmac [*sic*] indian
[*sic*] descent.

– [I] went to see a poor man who has been very ill for 7 months,
he and all his family belong to much despised & neglected race
called "Jack a Tars," they speak an impure dialect of French &
Indian, R.C.'s and of almost lawless habits.

– Jack-o-tar. A west coast Newfoundlander of half French or
Indian extraction.

– The Scots remained resistant to intermarriage with the French
for many years (although marriage occurred in increasing num-
bers), labelling the French "Jack-o-tars," a synonym for halfbreeds.

– Journois Brook, Shallop's Cove, and Bank Head, settlements
known on the West Coast of Newfoundland as the homes of the
"Jack-o-Tars," or "dark people" — the French-Indians.

– We met two Jackie Tar hunters from the West Coast and they
told us we would need a boat to cross the Humber River.

– A person on the West Coast believed to be of mixed French and
Micmac [sic] Indian descent; in recent decades an epithet refer-
ring to certain individuals of dark complexion, with a French
accent and intonation in their speech.

– There is a great quantity of eels and lobsters caught here, and in the winter the Jack-o-tars chiefly subsist on eels; they are a lazy, indolent people, and I am told, addicted to thieving; in the winter and spring they are frequently in very destitute circumstances; they are looked upon by the English and French as a degraded race, thence styled Jack-o-tars or runaways.

– The name by which deserters from the French Navy are known in Newfoundland.

– 1988 *Sunday Express* 24 Apr., p. 2. He noted that in the forties francophones [in Nfld] suffered discrimination and were labelled "Jackatars."

– 1881 *Evening Telegram* 26 Oct. One "jackatar" sympathetically suggested that a drop of "old tom" [rum] was a grand thing to steady one at sea.

– 1990 *Evening Telegram* 1 Mar., p. 28. In Newfoundland the French, for centuries living on the West Coast of the province, are still being referred to as Jackatars (I'm not sure what the term means, but everybody agrees that it is not a term of endearment).

Cedar Cove, Revisited
for John Steffler

No straight lines to square yourself.
Even horizon reads harsh — grey seas
butt shore and sky. Bearings taken from
the hunched back of Guernsey Island.

Here, hands were rough-hewn, akin
to volcanic coast. Digits of crag crammed
close, clamped on spades and hatchets,
mended nets. Clung to what little food this
shallow soil allowed. Nails worn blunt and
broken, bulged knuckles gnarled from
the brutal fusion of Earth's work.

Land this old knows better than to beg,
knows you'll come back hungry — questions
circling your skull like a flock of gulls.
Accept this rock, its odd love.

Oral History: Q and A (II)

Q: So, do you recall much about Crow Gulch?
   Like, any stories or experiences? Did you know
   anyone from there?

A: I knew a scattered one down there
   but only to see 'em. I mean, what ya hears
   and what ya knows can be a funny thing, right?
   Let's just put it this way — nothin' I really wants on tape.

Q: So you don't want to talk about it on record?

A: No, I can't say I do. Not with that thing on.
   You turn it off, and I'll tell ya a few things, though.

Escape

No way to heat this house at night.
Winter mornings, your breath gone
vapour. Frost on the bunk above you,
on the ceiling, pray the firewood's
not too damp. No fire, no buns and
molasses. Another hungry morning
of maths, standing next to your desk
reciting the Lord's Prayer — *give us this
day our daily bread.* But it's February,
and the bay's stacked with pack ice,
and this house lets in snow at the seams.

Bed's warm, though. Feather mattress,
all those freezing naked birds. Guilt.
You could sink down deep, cocoon.
And the weight of these homemade
quilts — you could sleep forever. Anything
but the bleary-eyed walk to the outhouse,
the small, cold shock of last week's news
against your skin. You could call it hardship.
All this hard living just to stay alive.
Nice to escape, though. This feather bed.
Dream up whatever life you want.

Ella Josephine Campbell

Slim, slight. Sinew and bird bones.
Cords of her hands like spruce roots.
Came from Ship Cove to Crow Gulch
with little more than the child inside her,

landed in a small shack flanked by
an outhouse, train tracks. Made it work,
had to. No surviving a place like this
without some acceptance, some yield
to the blunt force of what must be done.

Lived for a dance on the weekend, game
of Bingo during the week. Draped in her
favourite sweater, blue-green swirls on black,
three times her size. Costume pearls, earrings
to match. Heading to the Palace, all tobacco

smoke and last week's gossip. Nights she won,
she dropped by the Padarnac Lounge to chat
with her brothers, a quick rum 'n' coke —
warms the blood for the walk home.

Get her in the woods, she was all business.
Frantic flick of the rod whipping the hackle off
the fly long before trout ever could. Peals
of laughter against the far shore. No smooth arcs
or figure-eight false casts, just enough line
in the water to get wet. A woman most at home
without ceilings, without walls.

Influences

i)

Parson's Pond, The Arches,
Logger School Road, Bonne Bay,
Frying Pan Pond, Atlantic mackerel,
Copper Lakes, Nipper's Harbour,
Humber River, Mad Dog Lake, Brake's Cove,
short-horned sculpin, forget-me-nots,
Gros Morne, caribou, Lady Slipper Road,
Serpentine Valley, roseroot, Starlight Trail,
Buster Gough's Pond, Pinchgut Lake,
The Wreckhouse, brook trout, black spruce,
Little Port Head, Guernsey Island, balsam fir,
Joe Baggs' Pond, Table Mountain, Iceberg Alley,
St. Anthony Bight, black bear, Cook's Brook,
lowbush blueberry, Killdevil Mountain,
Spruce Pond, herring gull, Blomidon Hills,
partridgeberry, pitcher plant, Coppermine Cape,
Woody Point, spruce grouse, Norris Point,
Ten Mile Pond, Green Gardens, Arctic hare,
Rocky Pond, bakeapple, Bottle Cove, Burgeo,
Long Point, Bay of Islands, the Tablelands,
bald eagle, Marble Mountain, Gull Pond,
Signal Hill, lilac, Bell's Brook, Cape Spear,
grey jay, Man in the Mountain, moose,
beaver, tuckamore, Cedar Cove.

ii)

Skim-milk powder, baloney sandwiches,
snow through the gap in the doorframe
of our Dunfield apartment, frying chips
in lard on the stovetop, food-bank onions
and white rice in Ziploc bags, cans
of potted meat, cans of flaked ham,
cans of corned beef, cans and cans and
cans of _____, boxes of Kraft
Dinner, Mr. Noodles, Kool-Aid and Tang,
Plymouth Reliant Ks and Chevettes
with bench seats and only one mirror,
seatbelts still just suggestions,
trouting with uncles, all tough talk
and plaid jackets, fading blue-green
tattoos of crosses, nude women on their
forearms, couple sixers of Black Horse
in the canoe, not a lifejacket to be seen
between us, bags of one-cent candy
from the Corner Market, some family
friend behind me in line buying beer, cigarette
dangling from his lip, tightly permed
cashier offering him an ashtray,
eventually graduating from milk powder
to cans of evap, from Kool-Aid to frozen
cans of juice concentrate, *Cheers* and *Taxi*
on our black-and-white set, Letterman and *SNL*
in their prime, Fogarty telling the coach
to put him in centre field, Starship claiming
to have built this city from nothing more
than rock and roll.

iii)

Ralph Gough.
Occupation: blacksmith.
Cast himself roughshod,
some stoic, stony figure
to look up to. Served a stint
in the First World War.
Newfoundland Regiment,
number 781. Age: 21.
Early discharge for disorderly,
fit right in the Bay of Islands,
boxed bare-knuckle for sport.

Rudolph Gough Sr.
Occupation: wood-cutter.
Hands like bear traps, still
hand-rolled perfect cigarettes.
The odd hip flask passed around
with lunch, slabs of baloney
on mustard sandwiches.
A few coffee-can tea kettles
on a low fire, ten tea bags
to a brew, and the stuff's dark
as the Humber, strong enough
to strip bark. Spent his last decade
alone, mug after mug of weak tea
as he mourned my grandmother,
raised two grandkids as his own.

Rudolph James Gough Jr.
Occupation: labourer.
Gunnin' it through the Wreckhouse
dark to catch the night crossing,

a few hours sleep before the twenty
hours straight drive to Toronto.
Long before Fort McMurray flooded
our heads with dreams of more than
getting by. Always brought some odd
gift to mark his return home.
One year it was coins and bills
from French Guyana, the dollar
so thick, so real in my small palm.
Another year, a margarine tub
of saved change. A first edition
of some book neither of us had
heard of. The cover was embossed
leather, the lady he bought it from
claimed it came across and landed at
Ellis Island. I think on that feeling,
coming home after months away,
standing on the deck, approaching
Port aux Basques. Never so happy
to feel a bitter wind running you
through to the bone.

iv)

Both my grandmothers
have been dead for decades.
I am 36. My father's mother,
Ella, when I was 8, my sister
just months old. My mother's
mother, Marion, when I was 14.

I remember very little
of Ella, mostly being shy
in her kitchen, adjusting to
having these new people,
this new last name. Now,
all I have are old photos,
a handful of stories, one more
life-hyphen to live up to.

Her word was uncontested
in a home of men, all
mouths and puffed chests.
Foolish daytime-TV bravado.
She'd call bluff with one
sidelong glare from her seat
at the table, the slow smoulder
of a Rothmans driving home
the point without a word.

In a room of hot air
and soft bellies, fragile egos,
she was cast iron. I can't,
for the life of me, remember
the sound of her voice.

The more I write, the more
this breaks my heart.

Marion, for most of my life,
was ill. I'd stay with
her and my grandfather on
Saturday nights, attend church
on Sunday. I'd stare at the photo
of her at Rocky Pond, where
they'd camp on an island in summer.

She's sitting in their aluminum
boat holding up two gorgeous
brook trout, face betraying
the effort to hide her suffering.
At one point, she took one
of his tackle boxes to sort
and store all the pills it took
to keep her alive, some
of them still in test stages.

Hepatitis from a transfusion,
jaundice turned liver failure
turned liver transplant (turned
rejection and another transplant),
kidney failure then dialysis, then
the heart attack that took her
in the shower at 56. My mother's
voice when she got the call
still finds its way into my dreams.

I sit in this canoe (am I dreaming,
again?) to glean their voices from

the cries of crows, a breeze through
black spruce, an old leather Bible,
costume pearls, rewriting all the
long-dead stories we keep repeating
that keep us disconnected,

circling ourselves.

Fuck this town

This mill with all its money gone wrong. Fuck the cut-eyed stares and the stigma. Fuck the train and the tracks too, never done anythin' but make us into thieves to feed ourselves. And that school with all the Brothers makin' ya feel like scum, all the other kids from town learnin' to be just like 'em. If God don't want me, no one will. Can't even go up Broadway without bein' chased or spit on. Girls won't even look at ya 'cause you're from Crow Gulch. I swear, too, the next bastard that calls me jackatar's gonna get a good shit-knockin'. I just gets so angry with it all, I don't mean to cry, but it just comes out and then I feels stupid, like I betrayed me own feelings. Feels like there's somethin' wrong with me. Can't tell anyone around here that, they'd only think there was somethin' wrong with me, ya know? We're all too busy tryin' not to slide down into the bay to worry about that stuff anyways. I dunno, b'y, maybe I'm just talkin' outta my ass. Forget I brought it up.

Aerial Photo

Shacks squat against Crow Hill, dissected
by tracks, then tumbling to shore. Millbrook
Mall still just logpile. Pier Road, Corner Brook's
western edge of civility, buffers the rest of Town.
Gets only tail-end abuse — *only kiddin', b'y.*
Least you're not livin' down over the hill.

Bay's corner lies log-boomed, nondescript
shapes like crop circles. Ol' Bowater furious
when the boom would break, crowd from
the Gulch took whatever washed ashore, built
what they could and sold the rest.

A dozen dories point toward Guernsey Island,
a few more cling to shore. Tiny homes tucked
between boulders that dwarf dwellings two- and
threefold. Some outsize passing train cars.

Precious grids of Townsite houses, patterned
windows of the Co-op, Western Memorial,
the mill oozing affluence, indifference.

Funny, from up here it all looks so simple.

A Moment's Notice

The main track of the Canadian National Railway traverses the Pier Road and Crow Gulch areas and serves the latter as a somewhat irregular pedestrian access. [...] These tracks are within no clearly defined right-of-way and structures have been built as close as fifteen feet from the tracks.

The track became a symbol of loss
and gain. Billy's leg bad enough,
the young Baker fella got killed.
His mother with another one on the way,
almost miscarried with grief. Wreck
of '66 that took three lives, made
three more widows.

The train also dropped enough coal
to sell to the crowd up town who had
proper stoves. The more daring robbed
cargo cars as they slowed on the bend,
tossing off boxes of potatoes, sacks of flour,
now and then a fifty-gallon drum of stove oil.
Miracle, none of the drums crashed through
someone's kitchen, building speed until
they hit the bay.

The tracks were also road, sidewalk
and driveway, nothing to see a few young
fellas hanging off the back, hitching a ride
to Broadway. Over time the racket and rumble
became ingrained in daily life, a train's passing
became like the sun — brilliant and mundane
in the same go, able to destroy what
you know at a moment's notice.

Unsure

Livin' in Curling and going to Corner Brook,
you'd never go up the track because you know
you'd get a lickin'.

Coming up the track from Curling,
late for a hot date with a Townsite girl.
Young fella's all sweat and nerves,
bullets soaking through his collared shirt.
Pomade running off his ducktail haircut.

It's not the slow dance or that first kiss,
not the frantic chance of being felt up outside.
He's scared to death those jackatar bastards
will spot him, afraid the rocks and sticks
will come raining down on him. Sure enough,
he spots a kid about his age up on the hill,
hands balled into fists. Stone-faced.

The kid from Crow Gulch looks down
onto the tracks, remembers —

runnin' full tilt down over the stairs
past Broadway. Three older boys.
Clutchin' the new pair of loafers
that he'd sold stolen coal and firewood
to buy himself. Hadn't even worn 'em yet.
Down into the Valley, rocks raining down
on his back, and he falls hard, knocks
the wind out of himself. Breathless
and bloodied, he feels them standin'
over him. Feels the heat and hate
of spit hittin' his shirt, laughter like a knife

when one of them takes a shoe and tosses
it into Corner Brook Stream, says *didjya*
really think you was good enough
for them fancy shoes —

Through gritted teeth he curses the fella
from Curling in the collared shirt. Tries
laughing at his coifed hair, the nice shoes.
He half-hearts a couple rocks down onto
the tracks, tear-streaked cheeks hot with rage,
unsure if he feels hatred or brotherhood.

The Sea Is Always Happy

for Aaron Crossley

We fling ourselves upslope, ropes
strung between tuckamore like patio
lanterns kissing blisters onto our hands
as we force legs and lungs against
gravity, feet fixed to the steep
of Little Port Head like gnashed teeth.

Cresting the first hill, we're lulled still
by the sun, high and lonesome, patient
as a gunslinger. Hands arched over brows,
slammed with so much light we're thinking
death as much as life, we're interrupted

by a single crow,
by a small, tattered absence against blue,
by a Rorschach blot flossing the brain's fickle folds,
by an obsidian mouth unafraid of flesh,
by the elegant black gloves of a good death,

interrupted by this small reminder
that the cliff's face would beam at any
sudden impulse to jump, any small urge
to look away from the future's blank stare.

That the sea is always happy
to swallow you up in a wink and a smile.

Rudolph Gough

Built from bucksaws, lugging moose
meat. Wild-eyed for history, often knew
more about your family than you did.
His laugh like wolves' teeth over gravel,
topped with a gold canine. Idolized Louis
Riel, loved Tina Turner. *Thunderdome.*

Grew up cutting wood for Bowater.
Crew bosses always eyed him, one kept
trying to trade two of his own for Rudy
— *fella can stack a cord of wood quicker*
than I can roll a smoke. He just loved work.
Kept him strong, feeling useful.

A lifetime of plaid jackets, ball caps.
Hip waders and fly rod, wicker fish basket
over his shoulder. Same leather strap he'd
use for Ol' Angus come Fall, his father's
iron-sight .303 Enfield from the first war.

That nineteen-point bull in Area 5. Brute.
Had to cross the Humber on log booms,
two quarters on his back. Almost across
and he fell in. His brother caught his arm,
hauled him back up spitting and cursing
at himself for losing half the meat.

Ran with a hard crowd on Broadway.
Not one for fights but quick to bust a jaw
if need be. Haunted the Bucket of Blood
with the Campbell brothers who bounced

the Padarnac Lounge, kept the Harmon Base
servicemen in line.

His father, Ralph Gough. Ghost.
Blacksmith before the war,
bare-knuckle boxer after discharge.
Not so much stoic as grim.

The choice, here — choose something
tough as love or risk turning stone.

The City of Corner Brook will take title to 29.85 acres of land in the Crow Gulch and Pier Road sub-areas in order to implement the scheme. [...] This land should be sold to the city at 50 cents per square foot. The remaining land is unusable and is to be held by the city only to prevent any recurrence of Crow Gulch.

A Backward Glance

Dunfield Park, 1987. All the laddios
in denims, the odd Steve Miller band
T-shirt. The Eagles, Nazareth. Skin
long past burnt, flakes and strips peeled
and picked each evening between cigs
by girlfriends in perms, tight ringlets
like waterfalls against bare shoulders,
teasing skin into birdsong. Outdated.

Small fleet of Chevettes, K-cars, the odd S-10.
All painted Tremclad flat black, rolled on thick
between beers. Cases of Molson 50 stubbies
sweating on the floor, out of the sun. One of
the older fellas walks by, chats about the heat.
Offers a nip of Seagram's, to share a toke.
CCR's "The Working Man" keeps 'em all busy enough
not to notice they'd rather be trouting, rather
give in to this midday heat, dodge down
to the Corner Market for another doz-box,
pack of Du Maurier. Chat up the new cashier
with the Pat Benatar haircut.

Something about the colour of things,
then. Something mono, something VHS,
AM radio about it all concerning aspect
ratios. Pre-pixel. Something so believable
in its seeming impossibility — that we used to
smoke in hospitals, cars only had mirrors
on the driver's side, bench seating.
That someone was still considering the lunar

landing, still mildly amazed by colour TV,
how we ever got over two world wars.
Always letting go of what we know, how
we live on the future's brilliant, polished edge.

To accommodate rapidly increasing population it was decided in the early 60's that Corner Brook should have its own Churchill Park in St. John's. Sir Brian Dunfield was knighted by Great Britain not as Supreme Court lawyer and judge but for his brilliant leadership of the St. John's Housing Corporation, was made chairman of the Public Housing Authority of Corner Brook in 1965. It was not the judge's first look at the west coast city. Several years earlier he had expressed the opinion, in a speech at St. John's, that the best cure for Corner Brook's ills would be a large scale fire.

Ella and Rudy

She loved his swagger, the bigger-than-I-look
way he entered the room, somehow underlined
with respect. Found himself looking at his feet,
stealing glances. Nerves flooding his chest
when their eyes met. Her brothers teased
her for having a few extra beer to offer, anything
to delay his leaving.

Hard truth was she had nothing to her name
outside eight kids and a shack that let light in
at the corners. Didn't matter. He fell for her like a stone,
left the valley to start over. Loved the raw honesty,
how they earned every scrap. Eventually moved on up
to Dunfield Park, oil heat and running water
like winning the lottery.

After Ella died, he'd drink cup after cup of tea.
Always let the kettle scream a few minutes past boiling
as he blank-stared the kitchen window, us wondering
what he was waiting for, if he was going deaf. Kept
getting hit by cars. *Magnetic*, we joked, had to be.
Just different. Spent his last years like that. Deflated.

The few photographs of them together: kitchen
table, littered with bottles, ashtrays, stray playing cards.
Her slender hand holding a half-smoked Rothmans,
giant glasses magnifying her dark eyes, yet still outshone
by her grin. His thick hand draped lazily over her shoulder,
a wild look in his eye, ready to correct someone's local
history. She'd let him speak, then tell how it really happened.

Together in their favourite way —
surrounded by friends, stories.
Enough to keep tomorrow
at bay a little longer.

Killdevil

Scrambling scree nigh on fifty degrees
steep, the body switches gears, welcomes
the physics of geology. The mind rewrites
its usual mantras, lungs become fetish
objects as body hair starts following
the sun. You won't grow claws or horns
but those canines might crave a little use.

Imagine yourself as caribou, tempted
by lichen and sedge, hoofing it a little faster,
now. Shedding self-consciousness, surprise
yourself as you grunt with each breath,
teeth gnashed in a mad grin for the top.

As you crest the edge, eyes sharpening
against the first truly new thing you've seen
in years, you don't want to plant a flag,
won't build some half-assed urbanite Inukshuk.
It's time to do this proper — take a lengthy piss,
let every other animal know you're still here.

My Father and I, Fishing

Home was the center of the world because it was the place
where a vertical line crossed with a horizontal one.
— John Berger

Our old canoe nudges the pond's silver skin,
paddles pull through cloud-spackled sky
as we set hooks in the mouths of brook trout.
Breaching fish become bullseyes, hand-tied flies
flicked forward, then that flash of fin and splash,
rod buckled half-moon in reward.

I read this surface like scripture, recognize time's
slow fold in the drift of rivers, my grandfather's
face in the fleeting wake of paddle strokes, but
depth eludes me. I vie for this seat with my mother,
usually end up hoofing the shore, smiling quietly
while she outfishes my father. Her glee pealing
across the water like bursts of light.

It makes me ache for my grandmother's company,
wish I'd shared this boat with her, watched her
bird-bone frame form laughter mixed with the cry
of diving loons. I sit across from him, my coltish
potential fumbling to keep up. From this canoe
he's seen himself in the sky, geese flying
through his mind like seasons.

It should be noted that the city assesses Crow Gulch houses at a nominal value of $300 each.

Rudolph James Gough Jr.

Baby of the family, first born in hospital.
Namesake. Delivered by Noel Murphy, war
doctor turned town dignitary. Rudy never saw
a car until kindergarten, but used to the train
passing right by the house. Everything hardened
to scale. Left the Gulch at 6, ended up anti-bully
of Dunfield park. No friend went unavenged.
Got his teeth kicked in by two older fellas, chased
out of C.C. Loughlin for chasing someone in.
Loved underdogs, anyone having done without.

Idolized his father, such subdued strength.
Heard stories of Ralph's boxing matches, short
time in the infantry. Snuck into *Enter the Dragon*
a dozen times. Spent the day collecting bottles
to cash in at the Coke plant, stood outside the cinema
asking anyone old enough to bring him in. Hid under
the seats between screenings, got his money's worth.

Spent half his twenties in Toronto. Factories,
tobacco farms, the odd construction site. Still
laughs to himself when he hears Stompin' Tom's
"Tillsonburg." Always, a need to live up to lineage.
Raw eggs and free weights, *Rocky III*. The time
he tossed some punk clean over a taxi for starting
shit, or when the station wagon broke down, he pushed
it up Bayview Heights. Mom steering, white-knuckled
prayer against a heart attack.

By 25 he was built like a bank vault
but never left the house or hung up the phone without

telling his folks he loved them. Still kisses my cheek
in airports. Small town alchemist, still teaching me
the evolution of strength — how to live up to a name
so wrought with work, so heavy, now, with love.

Dunfield Park

I just think it moved the problem, really. The first thing they did was paint the houses all different colors, they weren't hiding them away or anything. Jesus, what they did was painted them and said, ok we took all the scum out of there and put them up there, look where they are. I dunno, b'y. It's a crime.

After looking at similar developments in Halifax and Ottawa, Sir Brian settled on a species of row housing, or town houses as they were now called, the units being distinguished from one another by coats of paint in varying bright colours. It was promptly nicknamed Jellybean Square, and was the first of a number of such subsidized housing developments later spread throughout the city. These town house rows unquestionably would become the slums of the future, but in the meantime they were a great improvement over the slums of the past.

Dunfield Park, Jellybean Square. The Bean.
Shithole, full of trouble and youngsters. Each one
of them carrying crosses in the form of stigma
down Citadel Drive and, depending on who
they bowed to, taking shit from fellow Catholics
at Presentation or the rest at C.C. Loughlin.

As their parents, aunts, and uncles were called
jackatars in the Gulch, kids earned their stripes
being called "beaners" or welfare kids. Dunfield
gave them mansions as far as they knew.
Electricity, running water, and indoor toilets
seemed to materialize as if from a dream.

Not even the corner store nearby could escape,

rebranded the Beaner Market (mostly by those
who'd never been near it). In fact, it became
the prefix for most things have-not — *Looka buddy's
Beaner-boots!* or *Time to scrap that Beaner-mobile.*
Then there's the old joke about Father's Day confusion.
The Bean becoming an entire town's punching bag.

Stand Up to the Devil

It's not that I think less of them. I mean,
I've never had the urge to speak to any
of them. I just didn't mix with that crowd.
No one really did. Sometimes they'd be up
on Broadway, no trouble to pick them out.

I remember them just looking grey, sort of
washed out. One young fella used to skip
school to shine shoes down on Broadway.
You'd hear all kinds of rumours, one family
down there's supposed to have twenty kids,
another's running rum and whores. Another
guy's got a makeshift boxing ring behind
his house, mostly old plywood, mattresses.
Takes on all comers.

I can't say either way. Wouldn't surprise me
but you don't know for sure, right? I know
in school you don't hear a word from them.
No fear of the teachers, stand up to the devil,
they would. I've never seen them start a fight,
but lord help you if you picked one. Half a dozen
of them stoppin' that, right quick.

Fear of Guns

He's up three games to one, playing
bank eight. Sinks a slick cross-corner
to make it four. *Appetite for Destruction*
floods the basement, mixes with hash oil
and homebrew. Hand-rolled smokes.

Bored of pool, he disappears upstairs.
I crack a beer, practice my bank shot.
Miss, try again, miss, try agai — *click.*

I look up, two hollow black eyes
stare holes straight through me. He throws
his head back and howls, smells fear
and grows taller. Slowly, I unfold my small
frame, raise my hands. It's simple for him —

reduce me to stuttering, begging, whatever
gives him power. He drags the moment out,
slow and sombre as an Easter service, then
casually points the shotgun at my head,
turns it side-on and reminds me —

*the look on your face and you're still
not gonna do anything about it.*

Geraldine Winifred Walbourne

Toronto born, city slick until
the family moved back home
when she was 15. Watched
the CN tower go up, got to see
Queen live in '78. Bohemian.
She looks like Princess Diana,
the light eyes and height, her noble
nose perfectly askew. Sculpture.

Back on the rock, living out
of a tent until they saved enough
to rent. Bathing in Grand Lake
until November, cold water
became laughable. Still sleeps
with the window open year-round.

Birthed a bastard boy at 22. Moved
back to Brampton, lasted a year
or two before flying home to face
her father — newly minted Pentecost
pastor. Friction. The boy's father
nowhere, despite child-support
court orders. Show me the money.

She found sitters, worked behind
counters, behind sewing machines,
behind ovens, behind our kitchen sink,
our stove, behind every piecemeal bi-
weekly paycheque turned place-to-live,
enough-to-eat, behind every scrap
of clothes that kept the boy warm.

At 24, she meets my father.
The night she meets him, she loses
her grandmother. Jokes about him
being cursed, bad luck. This young
buck from the wrong side of town,
his last name both preceding and dragging
behind him like a loose bootlace.
Bad fit. Long hair, denim, and cowboy
boots. A face like Bo Brady, but shy.

This is where truly I begin. Age 2.

She's still mercury to me.
Steeled against life's battery
of bills, deaths, family politics,
but her laughter is liquid light,
filling rooms to burst. Her mind
is magma, is scalpel sharp,
is Scrabble smart, is an eternal
summer solstice.

Her heart? Things of this depth
I'll simply never know.

Clearance in the Crow Gulch area and in the seaward parts of Pier Road can best be done by burning the structures in situ.

In Response

to a performance by Vuntut Gwich'in artist Jeneen Frei Njootli

Hum
          burrow

electric glitch-and-dirge turns liquid

ears adjust

vibrato grows   fades   reverb shakes the blood,
liberates long-dulled synaptic lulls   fades again,
grows deeper   shuts my eyes.

Then the beat.

The beat becoming beats
                        beating back to themselves   perpetual

and infinite path transcending the tactility of skin
feels somehow deep-sea
                            but also lunar

something internal   skull's interior as rudimentary soundstage
the brain a soft abacus running its first new numbers in years.

The heart freestyled as hoof beats
transmitting frequencies thought long dead back to life

beating rhythms
along the ribs
fragile cage housing love
opens up UP and I remember —

this body is cage but also receiver   body as conduit reaching
both backward and forward.

I begin to see   somehow feeling
affinity with permafrost   feeling
tundral darkness as comfort   half-moon
Labrador landscapes I've only read about

snow is hoof-heaved upward against silhouettes,
nondescript but for
                              legs   and legs   and legs

blood   and bone   and hoof   and heart woven into loops
arcing and filling a small black room like night sky
looping and building and   and   an —

landed back on my sad   dumb ass   disconnected but hungry
chest blown open
like a floodlight

with so much work left to do.

Growth

The axe. A sharpened fist churning out
woodchips and stumps. Its thick thud
and chop into balsam fir brought warmth
to my hands, friction thickened my palms
to leather. The best trees ran thigh thick,
enough girth to endure a few good swings.

Bits of bark would rocket from the trunk
in arcs like kicked-out teeth. I thought I loved
those trees; their scent, embodiment of patience
as payoff. I mistook them as opportunities
to unleash anger. Satisfaction from wedging
that steel edge into their soft spines, violence
I had no business with.

I still enjoy trekking the woods, thinking
of Babe and Paul, wondering how they felt
when they heard the scream of the first
chainsaw rip through their lunch break.
I still take the odd tree, mostly deadfall
for my father's woodstove but now,

when I strike a match to birch bark,
a certain shame washes over me. A small
wish to find my teenaged self, shaking,
standing over a felled tree, his jaw full
of baby teeth clenched tight. To look
openly at the anger and shame twisting
his face into burls, gently take his axe,
lay it on the moss, see if he needs to talk.

Trouting

Get a canoe. Something old, beat up
enough not to cherish. If you're serious about this,
prepare to wear it as a hat. Don't kid yourself
with bass-boat dreams, trolling motors, or livewells.
You've gotta learn to be silent, self-sufficient.

Think Thoreau. Think free-range organic
without the hype. Forget about goldfish
or those poor bettas building their bubble nests
in vain. These trout shall be pet-named *Lunch*
and *Dinner.* Set the hook with a quick jerk,
accept what must be done.

Forget trophies, you're after pan-sized fish
whose necks are broken with deft pressure
from your thumb. There will be blood. The eyes
are best bait, but you have to get the knack
of coaxing them from the socket unbroken
with nothing more than patience and barbed hook.

Don't be greedy; catch enough for a feed
then leave. Don't feel shame, cruelty doesn't enter
this equation despite PETA posters or misled
McCartney messages. This isn't about trout-skin
trousers or ice-floe photo-ops. This is intimate
knowledge of where your food comes from.

Interventions

of a minor sort. A mental or emotional sort. So caught up in a cyclical course of obligation and fear that you get small hits of dopamine from cancelling plans. Hiding at home, curtains closed. Phone off. Hoping to be rescued.

A Sunday afternoon spent visiting friends, crawling out of a three-week hole that's stretched out for two months. Explaining in person, finally asking forgiveness. Made aware of the egotism in this. The lost up your own arse in worry, can't see how you're hurting others kinda egotism. Offered mixed advice — *should is a dangerous word, stop telling yourself the same stories, you shouldn't put your friends through this, the simplest answer is usually the right one, feel it out, get out of your head, this is not your fault, trauma is trauma.*

I used to trust. I don't want to keep asking what happened. Everything happened, I keep it happening in my head.

Should vs. want. Fear vs. do. Fear vs. failure. Failure vs. not doing.

Not doing as an exercise in safety, self-restraint, and risk aversion.

Useless skill set of a severity of thought and feeling.

Oral History: Q and A (III)

Q: Do you think the teachers may have treated them unjustly?

A: Umm...I think it's a possibility,
   probably because of where they were from,
   but, you know, when I look back now, I realize
   that I never ever exchanged two words
   with any of those kids.

Q: There was just a clear distinction?

A: Yup, and God knows none of us were rich,
   but they were sort of the poorest of the poor.

I remember in my own family there would be threats, you know, if we weren't doing as well in school as we ought to be. My mother would say, You're going to end up in Crow Gulch if you don't pull your socks up. *That was threat number one. The other threat was that you'd end up being a waitress at a Chinese restaurant.*

I Dream of Moose

So real I can smell them, unmistakable
moss-musk mixed with a blood run hot.
Dull fur shakes off bog-muck, chunks
of pitcher plants between its toes, leaving
tracks somewhere between upside-down
hearts, the smell of forget-me-nots in spring.

The light is best described as dusk,
warm colours washed out. Things get
a bit serious. Not dire, just quiet.
Emerging from treelines (there's always
a treeline) in small groups, they're both
to scale and skewed. Mercurial limbs stretch
and shrink to tiptoe over bungalows,
limbo under street signs like liquid.

Cross four-lane highways in single steps,
navigate downtown cores. Flag taxis.
Then everything shifts, moves indoors.
They lose their hooves, dismantle
antlers and become one large non-moose
sitting in its old blue T-shirt, pair of
well-worn Wranglers. Non-moose has
grown a gold tooth and now has the power
of gravelled laughter, has grown a pair
of hands thick as slabs of granite.

Non-moose is your grandfather,
sitting in his bedroom. The one he spent
his last weeks in, his body falling away
from him in mutinous strides. He used to
throw his head back and laugh, throw

back Five Star and water, used to work
like a dog and smoke like the devil.
Used to love like an army of young
hearts off to war, lied about their age,
desperate to fight for something good.

This time my grandfather sits on a plain
wooden chair, backlit aside from his
socked feet, those bouldered hands.
Left kneecap catching light, forearms
folded, bristling with the urge to work.

Early this morning, before birdsong
pulled the sun up over the precipice
of another round of bacon and coffee,
gridlock, small talk of weather, before
the entire eastern seaboard hit snooze
a second time, this moose, this non-moose,
this now-man simply sat in his small room,
mostly darkness.

His voice wasn't out loud, not quite
in my head, either. More a resonance
in my bones, inhabiting marrow like code.
It scares the shit out of me, but I trust
these moose, these shape-shifting
shadows that reveal themselves in true
form. I trust him, his answer to questions
I never had to ask —

stay hungry

keep digging

be unsure and own it.

At First Glance

                    it looks like
he's standing shin-deep in water,
reeds yielding to the breeze in bands
of evening sun. His blue plaid jacket
hangs open, its tail in mid-sway
behind him as he steps back onto shore.

The photo's old, recklessly nostalgic.
Windswept black spruce fawning in golden
light, the pond's gentle chop a mix of silver
and sapphire, the canoe on his shoulders
so red you can't help but think of blood.

His eyes are lost in shadow but it's just
as well — it makes little difference if it's
his face, his mother's, my own image
looking back at the camera, caught
in the middle of something so imperative.

Emerge

Trail gives way to hard beauty, this
cliff-buffered cove. Plateau of earth
carpeted in roseroot, capillary spread
of juniper bush keeping things intact
before the rush and tumble to shore.
The gulf throws its thoughts at you in fits
and gusts. Stand. Lean long, long into
the wind, float on air's impossible arms.

Build a rock wall, scoop out space
for fire despite sea-shouts, the spray
that salts your skin. Fool yourself
into thinking you can keep things out
of their own homes. Ah! but flames
first shy soon speak in tongues, engulf
driftwood, their wicked lash and lunge
as wind translates, amplifies their ire.

Having sat out the sunset, eyes fixed
on the day's long fade, the sea goes grey,
rears on hind legs. Granite-faced with anger
on its sleeve. Light yields to the mean side
of this place, of all places, how darkness
sharpens its teeth against the fear
of any stony thing we can't bargain with.

You didn't even notice your tourist cap
blow clean off your head, useless suede
thing, its embroidered moose unravelling
as you broke from the trail, tumbling
across the field behind you. Slipping away
like a small fear overcome.

There is a wilderness that knows me better than I know myself.
— Robin Richardson

Acknowledgments

Land.

This book was written while living/studying on the territories of the Beothuk and Mi'kmaq peoples on the island of Newfoundland and the Syilx Okanagan Peoples in British Columbia. My umbilical connection to the former and the privilege of welcome, challenge, and education from the latter inform all steps forward — honest heart, open mind, straight spine.

When it takes nearly a decade to realize a book, you have a lot of people to thank. To the three who started it all — Stephanie McKenzie, Randall Maggs, and John Steffler — without your friendship and tutelage I'd never have gotten started. For access to invaluable research resources (including their own work) I deeply thank Rainer Baehre, Neil White, and George French. Huge thanks to Cecily Nicholson for truly seeing me and this project at the time when I doubted it the most. Matt Rader, for asking the tough questions and issuing the right challenges at the right times. Ashok Mathur for guiding me gently and honestly through the minefield.

Many thanks to Gregory Younging for seeing the intrinsic value of this book, for confidence and friendship, for everything you've done for publishing and literature in this country — rest easy, friend.

To dear friends on both ends of the country — there are, literally, too many of you to name, too many examples of how and why you deserve personal thanks — I am truly fortunate to know you all. Thank you for the deep conversations, the adventures over the bogs and through the hills, the workshopping, for all your love, laughter, and support. I wouldn't, couldn't, be here without you.

To those who generously granted me permission to use their work and research — I do not take this trust lightly, thank you.

To everyone at Goose Lane and icehouse, huge thanks for all the patience and hard work, for helping this dream become tangible. Julie Scriver — thank you for seeing what I see better than I ever could. To my editor, Robin Richardson — thanks so much for getting it, for understanding just what I was trying to do, and for a sharp eye when I veered off course. To James Langer's attention to technical detail and honest advice — much appreciated. Allie Duff, Heather Nolan, and Andy Woolridge — thanks for reading early drafts and writing poems I wish I'd written.

Several of these poems were previously published in the following journals: *Canadian Literature*, *CV2*, *Prairie Fire*, and *Riddle Fence*. Additionally, the poem "In Response" first appeared in the collaborative chapbook *Correspondence: real time + real distance literary exchange*. My thanks to the editors for taking a chance on my work.

I wish to acknowledge the following organizations: ArtsNL for financial support; the Writer's Alliance of Newfoundland and Labrador; the Newfoundland and Labrador Arts and Letters Awards; the staff at Corner Brook public library; the staff at the Ferris Hodgett Library; the Corner Brook Museum and Archives; Inspired Word Café; the March Hare Literary Festival, and The April Rabbit — 'ear, 'ear!

To my mother, father, and sister — I know I'm not always easy to be close with. I keep choosing poetry over practicality, yet you've always had my back. I know it, I feel it, and I can never thank you enough but know that I'll always try. I love you.

Lastly, to Crow Gulch — this story has become mine, too. I can only hope that through this book I've done it some justice. That we can remind Corner Brook that Crow Gulch was here.

Notes

The quotation in the introduction is taken from the seminal Newfoundland novel *House of Hate* (McClelland and Stewart, 1970), by Percy Janes.

The epigraph comes from John Steffler's *The Grey Islands* (Brick Books, 1985). The epilogue (in a slightly altered form with permission from the author) comes from Robin Richardson's *Sit How You Want* (Vehicule Press, 2018).

The found text on pages 13, 41, 49, and 58 as well as the poem "A Moment's Notice" take text directly from the *City of Corner Brook Urban Renewal Scheme*, published by Project Planning Associates Ltd., Toronto. Used courtesy of the estate of Macklin Hancock, author of the document.

The found text on page 44 comes directly from Harold Horwood's *Corner Brook: A Social History of a Paper Town* (Breakwater Books, 1986). The poems "Dunfield Park" and "Escape" also take text and inspiration from this title. Used courtesy of the estate of Harold Horwood.

Several of these poems are taken from/incorporate text from Dr. Rainer Baehre's Crow Gulch oral history research and the *Bowater Oral History Tapes*, including the found text on page 65, "Dunfield Park," "Oral History: Q and A" (parts I and III), and "Unsure." Used courtesy of Dr. Rainer Baehre.

"Aerial Photo" was written in response to a photograph of Crow Gulch housed at the Corner Brook Museum and Archives. Used courtesy of George French, the museum's archivist.

"Definition" is compiled from definitions and example usages found in the *Dictionary of Newfoundland English* (University of Toronto Press, 1982 and 1990). Used courtesy of the University of Toronto Press.

"In Response" was written after witnessing a performance by Vuntut Gwich'in artist Jeneen Frei Njootli. Used courtesy of the artist.

The epigraph for "My Father and I, Fishing" comes from John Berger's *And Our Faces, My Heart, Brief as Photos* (Vintage International, 1991).

"September 14, 1966" is a found poem from the September 14, 1966, issue of *The Western Star*, which covered the story of the Crow Gulch railway disaster. Used courtesy of *The Western Star*.

Poet. Newfoundlander. Mixed/adopted Mi'kmaw. Life is hyphenated.

Walbourne-Gough's father's family lived in Crow Gulch until the community was legally ushered out, mostly relocating to Corner Brook's first social housing project, Dunfield Park. Walbourne-Gough holds an MFA in creative writing from UBC-Okanagan. His poetry has appeared in *Riddle Fence*, *Canadian Literature*, *Prairie Fire*, *Newfoundland Quarterly*, *QWERTY*, *Forget Magazine*, the *Capilano Review*, and *Contemporary Verse 2*. *Crow Gulch*, his debut collection of poetry, was longlisted for the First Nations Communities READ Award. It was also a finalist for the Derek Walcott Prize for Poetry, the Raymond Souster Award, and NL Reads.

Photo: Heather Nolan, heathernolanphotography.com